Nick

AN ODE TO WOMAN

Hope you laugh and cry in all the right places ☺

An Anthology Of Poems Dedicated
To The Art Of Being A Woman

Enjoy the book ♡

and thank you ✗

Written and Illustrated by
Paula Love Clark

Love

Paula 🐝

Disclaimer

This book is designed to provide information and motivation to our readers. It is sold with the understanding that the author and publisher are not engaged to render any type of psychological, legal, or any other kind of professional advice. The content is the sole expression and opinion of its author. Neither the publisher nor the individual author(s) shall be liable for any physical, psychological, emotional, financial, or commercial damages, including, but not limited to, special, incidental, consequential or other damages. Our views and rights are the same: You are responsible for your own choices, actions, and results.

The content of the book is solely written by the author.

DVG STAR Publishing are not liable for the content of the book.

Published by DVG STAR PUBLISHING

www.dvgstar.com

email us at info@dvgstar.com

ISBN: 1-912547-40-6
ISBN-13: 978-1-912547-40-1

DEDICATION

Dedicated to my children Harriet, Lauren and Zac
And to my friends Isabel, Sara and Allie for always
believing in me.

AN ODE TO WOMAN

An Anthology Of Poems Dedicated
To The Art Of Being A Woman

THE TREE INSIDE OF ME 2

BARREN 3

GIVING BIRTH 4

SLEEP WHERE ARE YOU? 6

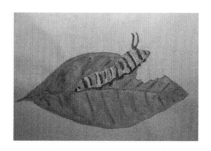

TIDDLY TODDLER 8

BEING FOUR 9

MOUTH SHUT 10

OPEN DOOR POLICY 11

HAPPY AS A TREE 12

LITTLE GIT 13

THE LONELY BENCH 15

THREE IS A CROWD 16

AN ODE TO THE BULLY: MARK 1 17

THE BLOOD 19

BOYS AND STUFF 20

BEING 14 21

SLUG FACE 22

I'M FINE REALLY. MARK 1 23

TEENAGE LOVE 25

ALIEN ABDUCTION 26

THE REBEL 27

EMPTY NEST 29

BOUNCING BACK HOME 31

FIRST DATE RULES: CONSUMPTION 33

FALLING 35

LOVE 36

SIZE DOES IT MATTER? 37

I'M FINE REALLY. MARK 2 38

FLIPPING TUMMY 39

SUGAR TITS AND FANNY FLAPS 40

BEHIND THE BUGGY 41

AN ODE TO THE BULLY: MARK 2 42

THE CHORE 44

MUMMY CAGE 46

THE SOUND OF YOUR NOSTRILS 48

MRS INVISIBLE 49

FORBIDDEN FRIEND 51

PECKING OLD HEN 52

AN ODE TO THE BULLY: MARK 3 54

HEARTBREAK 56

LULLABY.. 57

END OF MARRIAGE 58

DIVORCE 60

CHANGES: THE BUTTERFLY AFFECT 61

IT'S OK TO BE ALONE 64

OH DEAR... 65

LOST IN HEADSPACE 66

WRETCHED ANXIOUS SONG 67

DATING POOL 69

PANDORA'S BOX 70

I DON'T WANT YOUR MAN 71

THE WOMAN IN OUR STREET 72

DIRTY FLIRTY 74

BLOW OUT 75

SECOND CHANCES 78

TWO MANY WOMEN 81

THE BIG 5-OH 82

SHE'S A TENOR LADY 84

MENOPAUSAL ME 85

I'M FINE REALLY. MARK 3 86

MY PHONE CALL QUEEN 87

FUNNY LITTLE BESTIE 88

WOMEN IN ARMS 89

LADIES WHO LUNCH 90

MUMMY ROLLS AND FLABBY STUFF 92

SAYING GOODBYE 95

I SEE YOU 96

WHERE HAVE ALL MY TEA FRIENDS GONE? 98

I HAD A BLAST... 99

I'M FINE REALLY. MARK 4 100

FOREWORD

As I journeyed into Paula's world, I hoped these pages would never end, as I got to know Paula's mind; full of clever tricks to take the reader with her, into what I can best describe, as her witty world of charm, despair and intriguing motherhood.

Paula's life with open and closed doors, her once read, never forgotten approach to poetry, is undoubtedly raising a new bar that will connect with every walk of life.

When poetry is this good and thought provoking, as Paula's is, new readers will discover the joys buried deep in the pockets of her killer endings, leaving you with Paula's poem in your head for the rest of the day.

I can see Paula's writing becoming an anthem of life in these times.

Poet Steve Biddle, International, Glastonbury and Slam Award-Winning Poet.

ACKNOWLEDGMENTS

I would firstly like to thank my wonderful friend Isabel Morris for encouraging me to write and speak my poetry at her Dorking Is Talking poetry evenings. She saw in me what I was too blind to see at first. An incredible poet herself and I can't wait to one day be sharing a stage with her reciting our work together.

For Steve Biddle, a multi award-winning poet, for his incredible foreword, which made me cry and for his time and patience to respond to my numerous questions on getting my work into print.

For Philip Chan, Entrepreneur, Coach, Teacher, Mentor, Ten Seconds Maths Genius, Bodyguard, for his encouragement and stalwart belief in my capabilities. And for introducing me to DVG Star Publishing.

For Sara Martin and Allie Kay, who pick up the phone when no one else does! That female friendship is the reason I wrote this book. It is dedicated to Isabel, Sara and Allie and all my other female friends who I have been blessed to have or have known in my life.

To DVG Star Publishing – Mayooran Senthilmani and his wife Labosshy. I am so grateful for your belief in my vision.

To John F Photography, for patiently photographing my butterfly illustrations and the countless times he had to send the file to me!

Finally to my children – Harriet, Lauren and Zachary. For my teenage girls listening to each poem as I wrote them. Thank you for your love, patience, laughter and tears in all the right places. This book is for you and me especially.

INTRODUCTION

An Ode to Woman is a collection of poems exploring some of the life experiences of a typical woman. The book touches on some of the most profound, life changing, poignant and amusing aspects of being a woman. Covering themes from pregnancy and raising children, to love, loss and heartbreak; anxiety, menopause and the tricky highs and lows of the dating game.

An Ode to Woman, will have you laughing, crying and nodding your head in recognition. They are poems based on real women and our authentic experiences.

The book is peppered with illustrations of the lifecycle of a Monarch butterfly, because everything starts and ends somewhere.

All poems are my own. I have no one else to blame! Enjoy and share with others.

Paula Love Clark

Seed of me, grow
To be free, to know
That life is more than what you see

THE TREE INSIDE OF ME

There is a tree growing in me,
A seed attached to walls so thick,
No time to think,
It happened so quick.
This growing seed inside of me.

There is a tree that grows within;
Tiny, sapling, incongruous thing.
No form or shape that I can see;
This little thing inside of me.

There is a tree inside of me,
That brings my heart alive with glee.
A beating heart beside my own,
Waiting with patience to be born.

This tree that grows inside of me,
Branching out with limbs that grow,
And breath in lungs that have yet to blow.
This growing seed inside of me.

There is a tree I will soon see,
A tree that grew inside of me.
A tree that soon will stand alone,
And sing his or her, own song.

And I am bearing this said tree,
The one that grows deep in me.
My skin expands to make the room,
For this growing babe to flower and bloom.

BARREN

I have a space where no place grows,
I have a space that has no toes.
That space was not meant for something new,
That space where nothing precious grew.

I have this space inside of me,
That never got to grow a tree,
That didn't grow a beating heart.
Not my mission, not my part.

GIVING BIRTH

Making lists, packing bags,
Tummy stretched, with marks so bad.
Waters break and in I go;
The feeling deep and the time so slow.
In waves and crashes come the pain,
Over and over and over again.

Gas and air make me sick;
Epidural isn't quick.
Tens machine a tingly sorrow,
Will it all be gone tomorrow?

Midwives come and then they go,
But not you babe, you're stuck and slow.
Threats of cutting as I cry
In agony out and asking why,
I chose to do this wretched thing,
And then I see my partner's ring.

We chose to have another life;
To build our team
Through troubles and strife.
And so I push with all my will,
Swearing hard and screaming still.

Epidural not kicked in,
To save me from my cursing sin.
Squeezing hands and rising up,
I'm close to quitting; giving up.

Cut me open, get it out,
Through the curtains of my open gut.

And then with one last desperate push,
I hear a mewl and so I hush.
Chaos in the room abates.
They see her head, she's through the gates.
One more hellish, tormenting grunt
And out pops, my girl, a scrawny runt.

She's pink and bloody and covered in stuff
And my body collapses; had enough.
And just before I faint and sleep,
I hold this bairn and breathe in deep.

Her baby smell it fills my air
So still, the pain, no longer there.
I'll forget and repeat again,
And banish the memory of this childbirth pain.

SLEEP WHERE ARE YOU?

Where has it gone?
Where could it be?
I had it before and now it's not seen.
For years it was there
And now it has left.
My eyes are so dark
And I am bereft.

Did you eat it? I ask and cry,
Feeling numb and with foggy eyes.
For it's gone and you are here,
So I guess that you ate it and that's not fair.
Yet you look so demure,
In your pink and your white,
But you gobble all my sleep,
When you cry through the night.

Munch away tittle one
Fill your heart and fill your tum
Fatten up your little boots
You'll soon forget your crawling roots

TIDDLY TODDLER

Ickle, lickle girl why take so long,
To walk from school singing your song?
Over and over and stopping to pick,
Flowers, plants, stones and stick after stick?
You poo in your pants, refusing to try
And word after word ends in why.
The same Disney film plays on a chain.
How could you watch it again and again?
You tire so easily
And rest in my arms
Wriggling and giggling
And I long for your pram;
When as a babe, I pushed you about.
No toddler that screamed, or a tantrum to shout.
Little girl as you sleep in the bed beside me,
And look to awake, when it quarter to three;
I study your face as a sweet babe you lie,
And the tears start to flow as I find that I cry.
These moments will fly and soon you'll be free,
But until then sweet child, stay here forever with me.

BEING FOUR

Curly hair and ickle white teeth
Flowery dresses, big girl pants underneath.
No need for nappies and dummy has gone.
Loves playing with tea sets, sings teddy a song.

A laugh in the park as I get pushed on swings,
I giggle and dance and love pink, pretty things.
Plastic beads, puzzles and dolls
Painting, drawing and bright coloured trolls.

Holding hands with my bestie and laughing in twos,
Disney, mermaids, glitter and dressing up shoes.
National Parks and days out running and free,
Rolling down hills, grazing a knee.

Bath times and bubbles, dad reads a book
We snuggle together, his shoulder a snook.
I go to bed smiling, so much love for my day;
A little girl happy, so much love came my way.

MOUTH SHUT

Close your mouth, eat your food.
Pick up your fork, get out of that mood.
Wipe your bum, wash those hands
Or germs will germinate and land.
Brush your hair, clean those teeth,
Get out the plaque from underneath.
Eat your greens, munch less sweets,
Or I'll take away your toys and treats.
Be polite and then be still;
Children and their wilful will.
Looking smart and being quiet,
Not jumping up and causing riot.
Go to bed and don't you fart,
I'll be having none of that,
Come here now;
Don't you shift
You're far too heavy for a shoulder lift.
Nagging, bugging, crazy child
Go to bed, so I can hide.
And when you sleep
Up I'll creep
And miss my angel and cry so deep.

OPEN DOOR POLICY

I remember when doors stayed shut;
When privacy was exactly that.
I peed in peace, pouring over a book
Now I crave that short spaced nook.
We can't keep locks since the kid got trapped
And we broke down a door as the crying babe napped.

I'd love to poo in peace;
Brain disengaged and mouth shut tight,
As I pushed out the remnants of the curry last night.

Ah the bliss to have some time,
To wax my legs. How sublime.
To bathe before midnight,
Where I then fall asleep.
Thankfully the tank wouldn't allow for too deep.

Oh for a simple locked toilet door
Without someone begging to come in once more.
And loo rolls not empty or towels placed straight
And nobody yelling 'Mum I can't wait!'

I know those days will come
And I will be free to pee in peace,
But for now I'm grab a second mum,
Straining quickly to release.

HAPPY AS A TREE

He loves to bounce and jump and run
And swing and climb; so much fun.
Building stuff and tearing down,
Acting up, being class clown.

What a joy a brother is,
What a thing to have as a sis.
A noisy, crazy, loud mouthed boy.
Please Mama, can instead I have a mermaid toy?

LITTLE GIT

You dirty little muffin,
You mucky little Joe,
I saw you nick Nutella,
First with fingers then with toe!

You scruffy little 'apenny,
You naughty little git!
I saw you not wipe your bum
And cover pants in it!

Oh brazen little charmer,
Oh waxing little champ;
If I had my way you'd be in jail,
For breaking my best lamp.

My swinging, flinging monkey.
My growling mewling cat.
I've got you now forever,
So I'm guessing that is that.

I know this time will pass
And one day you'll be grow'd up,
But I would swap you for a dog right now,
Or the sweetest, cutest pup

I'm only really joking,
You know I love you Stu,
But because you are a little git,
Half of this is true!

Life is hard and you don't know why
You want to crawl, then hide and cry
And asking how,
Growing up is oh so hard to do?

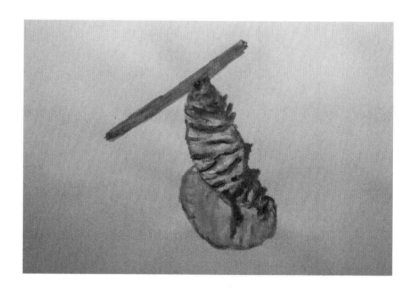

THE LONELY BENCH

That dreaded bench in playground sits,
For those with no friends, or warts or nits.
All by itself a place of fear,
Sitting by oneself, with no one near.
Where warriors and popular alike,
Or those with a fancy scooter or bike,
Would never go, as far too cool,
The best of the bunch they are at school.

Walking home I chat with mum,
How was school? Was it fun?
Sure I say with fibbing stench;
No heart to say I'd stayed on bench.

THREE IS A CROWD

I'm no longer your friend.
No longer fit in.
Not sure why, you didn't explain.
Is my hair too curly, or my clothes not right?
You were fine with me playing, at the park just last
night.
A new girl has started and she seems really cool,
And you seem really happy when you see her at school.
You make her loom bracelets
That you used to make me,
And I know that you asked her
Back home for some tea.
Everyone likes her and me too; she's nice,
But you're cold on me now, your friendship like ice.
I am no longer funny, no longer so hip.
I heard you tell Emma, I heard it slip.
We could all play together, you her and me?
No you say strongly, just me and her; not us three.

It's lonely at nine when your best friend has gone.
When she is laughing and singing your favourite song,
With another girl that isn't you.
This is the worst part of being a kid in school.

AN ODE TO THE BULLY: MARK 1

You stop me in the playground,
You step on my new shoes.
You pull my tie to choking tight
And my hair until I'm blue.

I cannot tell the teacher,
For you are teacher's pet
And I do not want to fight you,
For my muscles aren't there yet.

I do not tell my mother for she will go all sad
And I know there will be anger, if I tell my dad.
Instead I hide inside me,
Instead I've shut right down
And where once I was so happy,
Sadness wears the crown.

Childish me is leaving,
Goodbye I say.
We had fun though right?
Memories for another day.

THE BLOOD

My breasts are knots, small and pert,
So little flesh for so much hurt.
Tummy cramps, moods galore,
I don't know this me I wasn't before.
Tears they flow; they cannot stop.
Then without warning I laugh in a drop.
Friendship issues, nothing's right;
Why does my life feel such a fight?
I grab my dolls, when doors are closed,
I brush their hair and change their clothes.
Clinging to the childish me,
Yet mourning as I watch her flee.

BOYS AND STUFF

An ode to the boy, who touches my child;
I may be sweet, but a tiger inside.
She's growing up and has yearnings too,
But that doesn't mean she'll give out to you.
I'm being cool, but with sharp owl eyes.
I see the way you hold hands and smile.
Her neck with hickies bears the sign,
Of times to come where she'll be more yours than mine.

BEING 14

I giggle but have un-bearing pain,
I laugh but then I cry again.
My bum is small, I want it round.
Kim K, Beyonce, J-Lo all sound
Off, about their bum that's round.

My unearned money goes on creams,
To replicate a face of social media dreams.
I post a selfie, two or ten.
I stand in sunshine and pose again.

My hair is sleek and ironed out,
My lips a Benefit painted pout.
Eyebrows like slugs, skin is tanned,
St Tropez on carpet, Mum has banned.
The boys want stuff,
The girls all gossip.
Sometimes I cry inside my closet
Of skin-tight jeans and crop topped tops.
And yes I want it all to stop.

My phone it bleeps from wake to sleep,
I put it down and still it cheeps.
I yearn for sleep, but my head is full
Of angst and blues and snapchat drool.

Melancholy music plugged in loud,
I'm a Billy Elish fan in a Billy Elish crowd.
Where have I gone and who will I be?
I don't know. I'm only me and just 14.

SLUG FACE

I don't know how to tell you,
I know you'll just freak out,
But there's something rather weird,
That you should know about.

Your face has grown an extra;
A part that don't belong
And it's dark and big and bold and black
And looking simply wrong.

You say it's just the fashion,
That Kim K and all them do.
That I need to get with programme,
As I'm nowhere near cool.

Now maybe I am old
And way behind the times,
But since when did slugs become eyebrows,
With flicks that look like slime?

I'M FINE REALLY. MARK 1

Who am I? What's life about?
I'm fifteen years old and want to shout.
I'm flat, then up, then down again.
A repeating pattern in my brain.
Lost in my phone, other people's spaces,
Hiding from now, in social media places.
Love Island addiction, is quite a sin,
But reality stuff it draws me in,
And away from the mundane life that I am in.
But please don't fret or worry so,
I'm fine really. Fine. Just so so, so. so.

Emerging from the darkest place
I found myself a different space.
Who is this me anew?
And am I still the me I knew?

TEENAGE LOVE

My girl I watch you wash and wax
And preen and prance in mirror.
Benefit lips, Mac mascara,
Tea tree spots and tears,
Thing thong knicks that catch my breath;
I unload to God my fears.

You say you'd tell me if too close you came,
But somehow that talks seems oh so lame.
Semi-woman, loss of child
Growing up and growing wild.
Away from me you quickly walk;
Our words become like grown up talk.
But warning words I say to you,
Because I know it to be true...
Beware the cocky, floppy, spotty boy,
That sees you as a right of passage toy.

ALIEN ABDUCTION

I swear I left my girl in bed,
When I turned off all the lights,
But then awoke to find her gone
And left one that isn't right.

This alien her from Planet Crap
Is all that I have got;
She swipes and snipes and never smiles
And her bedroom smells like rot.

She uses all my face stuff;
She never washes up,
And she's using awful language,
Like bitch and hag and crap.

I really want my kid back,
The sweet one who made me cards.
Not this alien thing that screams all day
And cackles when she farts.

Please bring me back my angel.
This devil's gone too far.
She's nicking all my favourite socks,
So she can stuff and fill her bra

Aarggh I demand right now a refund!
I never signed up for this.
Please give me back the other child,
This one takes the p...

'Yes dear, Mummy's coming!'

THE REBEL

Drink and drugs and all things bad,
This rock n roll lifestyle is so damn hard.
I don't fit in, not a child no more,
But don't leave me crying at the grown up door.
Too young to vote,
So I walk with feet.
Slamming doors in rage retreat,
To others arms who welcome in,
The woman-child me that I've become.

Dolls and games don't fit my life,
Hanging in parks just bring more strife.
KFC, MaccyD and Subway;
My nutritional haunts and places I play.
I fill my lungs with vapes and tar,
Drinking vodka from a jar.

Siblings annoy me, Mum just nags.
Living my life is a daily drag.
But in bed at night when the air's not blue,
My silent, child tears crave Mama cuddles from you.

The choice is mine
Freedom. The choice; sublime

EMPTY NEST

I watch you pack, displace your strings,
I yearn to hold your childish things.
The teddy from a babe you've clasped,
Left on bed; I hear my gasp.
'What?' you say and tut your teeth.

I feel a rage that sits beneath
The motherly love I wear on face.
Really this is such disgrace!

How can you go, after all this time?
The times we've shared that were yours and mine.
The puzzles and books, playdough and beads,
Pushing on swings and planting of seeds.

Baking cookies and painting pictures,
Shopping sprees and parents evening teachers.
Crying together at soppy films,
Driving you to practise, parties and things.

And now you are leaving your mother's arms,
Leaving me with your plastic charms.

I'm proud of you, I know you know.
Like a mantra on repeat I tell you so.
Mature and focused, goals to achieve,
Yet I really do not want you to leave.

Stay here with me and we'll figure it out.
I'll be your taxi when you shout.
I'll make you tea and iron your shirts
Listen to your stories and soothe when it hurts.
We'll go shopping, have coffees
And lunches out;
Gossip and giggle. And I'll never shout.

Don't go. Please stay.
I scream inside.
I want you always by my side.
'I'm ready Mum! We've got to go.'
You say to me in words, tender, slow.

I know. I know. I know.

BOUNCING BACK HOME

Bouncy ball student started to bounce,
Once twice a month back into my house.
After the studies, came travels galore,
But the monies ran out and then you were poor.

Bouncy ball girl, you bounced back for a treat.
That's what you said, 'For only a week'.
Then bouncy ball girl saw the weeks just roll on;
No job was coming, my nagging a song.

Washing in basket, fridge no longer full
Eating it empty as a slip of a girl.
Taxiing mother, at beck and at call;
You want all my time, you want it all.
No longer a baby, no longer at school,
No longer adhering to Mummy's house rules.

Oh sweetness, oh light, oh love of my womb,
Why does the house feel so out of room?
You bounced towards uni without looking back
And you bounced back on home
And I'm feeling the lack,

Of my space, of my life, of being alone,
Of talking for hours with you on a phone.
Of lounging around, with no one to see,
Of leaving door open, when I go for a pee.

Fruit of my loins, result of sweet sex
I long to say goodnight just with a text.
Instead here you are and it seems that you stay,
But please find your bounce and bounce out one day.

FIRST DATE RULES: CONSUMPTION

Don't eat a donut with too much jam,
Or a crusty sandwich with chewy ham.
Forget the milkshake you have to slurp,
Or the fizzy drinks that make one burp.
Hot dog with onion will make you smell,
If not on your first date, then next day like hell.

Crisps are crunchy and finger licking fun,
Though not if you are watching the other eat some.
Coronation chicken will drip on your clothes
And your breath will leave him with upturned nose.

Oysters are iffy and prawns are a mess,
Beef if it's bloody will just stain your dress.
Tomatoes are squirty, leaves are no joke,
That cover your teeth and can cause you to choke.

Chilli is hot, curry is spicy.
Tastes great at the time,
But your bum smells less nicey.

So what should one eat on a first meet up date,
To create the right ambience, for meeting a mate?
To what sort of meal, should I sit down with you,
If everything's ruled out, from burgers to stew?

Chips. Let's eat chips with lashings of salt
And ketchup with mayo, what is there to fault?
If I drip or I slurp, you'll forgive me I'm sure,
And we'll moan in delight as we order some more.

Sweet love, to you I give my life.
You be my king and I may be your
wife

FALLING

I fell. Under your charming spell.
In a pub, over a pint of cider.
June hot days, when college was over.

How could I have known,
You'd be the one to share my life?
Someday you'd be hubby and I your wife.

Finding love, light and joy,
Over a pint of Bulmer's Dry.

LOVE

You blew my mind, wild.
With heart pinging, flipping, craving,
Longing for desired love.
I sigh.

Your words of hope, joy, future bliss,
Together with that fireworks kiss,
I melt.

You swept me, hooked and fed me
With what I lacked.
How did you know?
How could you see?
The heart shaped hole that resided in me.

That flipping, pinging heart of mine,
Betrayed by one's contagious smile.
And so I, choose to stay with you,
And that heart shaped hole filled with you stuff glue.

SIZE DOES IT MATTER?

I'm new to this sex stuff, it's really true.
And then I find myself with you.
Blue.

Where are the fireworks and romance of films,
The Carey Grant looks; suited men with their charms?

Instead I find myself a guy,
That leaves me asking why oh why?

If sex is so great and a thing of great pleasure;
Something to yearn and crave like lost treasure?

How come I feel no joy,
At the touch of this twenty year old boy?

With his dingly dangly, floppy bit,
That finds my enclosed knicker wrapped... area.

And I am left with feelings of remorse
And disappointment at his less than horse,
Sized thing.

Not quite what I was expecting.

I'M FINE REALLY. MARK 2

My life is a juggle, chaos resides,
Fine on the external, but not the insides.
Working long hours on my now chosen path,
Life all mapped out, one, long drawn up graph.

Met a guy and moving in,
Goodbye single life, there's a baby within.
But I'm fine just fine, with this solid blue line.

Baby drops out, wasn't quite ready,
Just eight weeks in, so I'm feeling unsteady.
Tears and grief and mixed up remorse,
Knowing stuff takes its own natural course.

I'm fine really. Just fine.

We're taking a break, needing some space;
He's moved on in and I'm not at our place.
Mumma she holds me and down I fall,
Yes this girl broke, after baby and all.

Fine. Not fine. Just taking my time.

I get back on up, us women do;
We get back together, so now we are two.
This guy I will love for the rest of my days,
Babies will come and some they will stay.

I'm fine really. Just fine.

FLIPPING TUMMY

First the look and then the smile,
I only had to wait a while,
Before the kiss.

Eyes on fire, sexual desire, locked.
And in that moment, I was hooked.
Your fishing line smile reeled me in,
Lost in the comfort of your wanting grin.

Faces inching closer,
Losing my resolve,
To hold back, off, away,
Save this intimacy for a further day.

Closer, inching, yearning, leaning, burning,
Desire.

I feel, sense, smell your breath,
Descending as chest on chest, we meet.
Our lips they greet.

Softness, then encroaching, yearning,
Arms around my waist;
Kisses deep in haste.
No longer feeling chaste,
I submit. Melt. Fall.

Under your manly promises of great times for all.
And I am lost under your spell,
To a mini-lifetime of your alcoholic hell.

SUGAR TITS AND FANNY FLAPS

The title says it all.
I think that's all to say.
So I'll let you run your mind amok
And your imagination play!

BEHIND THE BUGGY

Do you see me, that body with arms?
Pushing my child in her sweet, navy pram?
Shopping in basket, I live in my head,
From waking to sleep, I dream of my bed.
I average 5 hours of broken up sleep
So excuse me for losing myself in the deep,
Darkened cave, that lies in a space,
I've hidden in layers behind my dulled face.

Baby at weeks, is sucking me dry
I'm wretched and worn out and wanting to cry.
I'm giving and giving and not getting back.
Hubby don't get it, just mourning the lack,
Of loving from me, of nurture and sex.
I'm feeling lost and he feel like an ex.

I want to try more, to give him my all,
But the baby she cries and I'm up with a crawl.
Though I love her this sweet thing,
With all of my soul.
I'd die for her now,
This I do know.

But I'm lost and I'm lonely,
Don't know who I am.

So stranger, please, smile at this cracked nippled lady,
Dull, unshiny, unsmiling,
Who pushes that pram.

AN ODE TO THE BULLY: MARK 2

'Come into my office'
Words I could not bear.
My heart would sink, my stomach knot,
As I swivelled off my chair.
'Sit down!' came the instruction
And I would find a seat,
Feeling hot and sweaty,
In my self-destructing heat.

The crime did not befit me,
It wasn't something great.
Yet it caused you so much anger
And I felt the vibe of your pure hate.
As you growled and finger pointed
And made me feel like poo.
I wondered why this happens?
Did this happen to you too?

I wish I had the gumption,
The balls to say 'no stop!'
To put an end to how I felt,
With one karate chop.

Instead my tongue was stuck,
To the voice inside my head
And my shoulders sank into my back
And my heart it filled with dread.

And when the end had come
And my humiliation spent,
I'd have a little bathroom break
And allow my tears to vent.

You shouldn't do this thing to me,
I'm really rather kind
And a better employee,
You will struggle yet to find.

But find you must, I say,
For I cannot cope no more;
You've bullied me one too many days
And I'm walking out the door.

THE CHORE

I'm hiding in the bathroom,
I hope he doesn't know.
I'd hate for him to feel bad
When it isn't him you know.

I'm kinda really tired,
Worn weary by the day
And the last place I feel like being,
Is with him making hay.

I think we did it last week
Or perhaps the week before?
It may have been last month;
I've lost track like that before.

It used to be so cosy,
And all that welcome stuff,
But I feel like giving up on 'it'
I've really had enough.

He no longer wants to please me
And I never really try.
And when we do, I plan my shop,
It's true, I can't deny.

'But what if I was Brad Pitt?'
He'd say with a grunting huff.
'I bet you'd want to do it then
If he was in the buff?'

Mmm, I say a pondering,
As he tapped into my thoughts.
If you were Brad, I must admit,
I wouldn't wear my socks!

MUMMY CAGE

The Octopus Lady came one day,
'My word!' she exclaimed in utter dismay.
Dishes to wash, clothes to clean,
Surfaces to clear and then to glean.
Socks and pants left on floor,
Towels hang on every door.
Beds unmade and sinks unwashed,
Where the hell is that blue dishcloth?

Light bulbs to change, grass to cut,
Where is the man for things like that?
Fridges to fill and cupboards too,
Ingredients to buy for oxtail stew.
Letters to write, bills to pay,
Already taken half the day.
Trip to the shop, then to the bank,
Flower for a neighbour she has to thank.

Kids to school and back home again,
Homework to do to wrack the brain.
Supper to make, chips n' egg will do,
No one wanted oxtail stew.
Fill up the dishwasher and then unload,
This woman's feeling really bored.
Husband home and supper to eat,
Had a hard day love, massage my feet?

Baths to run, stories to tell,
No time to breathe in this mummy hell.
Kids asleep, so time to sort,
While husband grunts and farts and snorts.
TV time, with beer in hand,
He snores on couch in happy land.
She doesn't wake him, but pours a wine,
It's nine just gone: Mummy time.

Octopus Lady retires for the night.
No one screaming, no kids in fight.
Soon he'll awake and she'll engage,
But for the briefest moments,
She's free from the Mummy Cage.

THE SOUND OF YOUR NOSTRILS

Your snoring keeps me up at night.
Not ghosts or ghouls or terror frights.
Not money woes or stressful cares,
Just your bellowing sounds of nostrils flared.

It wakes the cat, disturbs the dog,
Who without you home, sleep like logs.
The kids are woken with moans of 'Dad!'
When did your snoring get so bad?

Would I have stayed early on in,
When two lusty people made different sin?
When we slept so sound and spooned together,
Awoken only by Britain's stormy weather.

What was the thing that happened to you?
That makes me so wrecked and feeling so blue?
The bags that now hang beneath eyes that once shone;
Dark, wretched circles, proof of your song.

The one that keeps me up at night,
Where I leave the room and that's not right.
I lay with the dog and the cat snuggles in,
As we await for dawn rise bemoaning your din.

MRS INVISIBLE

Do you still see me?
The girl you met so young?
The one who made your face light up,
With laughter, love and fun.

Do you still remember,
How you promised me so clear,
That you would always love me
And always keep me near?

Now you rarely see me,
Not as the person I once was.
More like a once new sofa,
Aged and hanging round the house

I had my hair done Friday,
But you didn't say a word
Instead you watched the TV
And said the football was absurd.

I bought myself a new perfume
And lost a bit of weight.
I joined a gym, got a tan
And watched the calories that I ate.

I got a little job,
In an office in the town.
I made some funny laughing friends
And didn't feel so down.

There's one there in particular,
A guy I like a lot.
His wife and him divorced last year,
But you still don't see a lot.

I started working later,
I started feeling fine,
And wondered if you noticed
That I'm singing all the time?

Then the day came that I left you.
The day came oh so quick,
But you didn't really care
You hardly really blinked.

You were also seeing someone,
A couple years before,
And your love for me had flown back then
And out our marriage door.

I wish you hadn't told me
And still I wish you'd also said,
Because I hate to think our love had died
And we slept together head by head.

FORBIDDEN FRIEND

We shouldn't be we, you and me.
You are with she and I with he.
Yet here we are you and me,
Not just two, not just three,
But four in this mess which brings no glee.
Forbidden friend it's time to go,
From me, or him, or her.
I know, you know, I know.

PECKING OLD HEN

There was a not very old woman who lived with you.
Two kids together, this is very true.
She cooked and she cleaned,
She smiled and she shagged;
Bless her for dressing up,
When her breasts were all sagged.

Her job went on hold, held back a few years;
Losing her status, she swallowed those fears.
The park and the group she took her kids to,
Then soothed all your woes when listening to you.

Talk of your job and your worry filled days,
And nodding abstractly when she spoke of kids play.
Once she held meetings and ran teams of ten.
Now she feels more like a pecking old hen.

But good times are coming,
A new space unfolds.
She's found passion in baking
And some she has sold.

Brownies and cookies, cupcakes and flans,
Her life has a meaning; her life has some plans.
So what will you do, now she's buzzing around?
No longer in mourning, for a life gone to ground.

No longer devoted to just you and them,
No longer being a pecking old hen.
Grab onto her coat tails and ride on her wave,
She's moving quite quickly for she is quite brave.

Walk with your woman and run alongside
For you joined up together for this married life ride.

AN ODE TO THE BULLY: MARK 3

In the beginning, was love, lust and joy.
Then I birthed a girl and after a boy.
You started to get sad and really rather blue,
But wouldn't share your thoughts as I would do with
you.
You started drinking heavy
And then the fear set in.
Creeping, sliming, sticky stuff
That only stuck within.
At first your words were mocking,
Lightly so at first,
But then came downright nasty tones,
But still you had a thirst;
To put me down in public
And put me down at home
And soon I believed all you said
And what was left of me was gone.
Creeping, sliming, sticky stuff
That filled up all of me
And soon I oozed out sadness,
Like a weeping, willow tree.
You said I love you baby
You said it all the time,
When punching walls, or smashing chairs;
Yet you didn't see the crime.
How strange that one who loves me,
For better or for worse,
Is the one who caused me so much pain;
The bully in this verse.

Fragmented, broken torn apart
I watch you leave my wretched heart.
And when you go, you leave with me
A tattooed stain that I will always see

HEARTBREAK

Cracking, splintering, aching heart,
Wretched, crying, bleeding, disintegrated,
Pounding, yelling drum.
Beating, yearning, dulled and broken,
A symbol of my love; a token,

That you stole with needy, greedy hands.
Swore blind you would protect it.
Instead you cut it clean in half
And sorrow came and ate it.

Promises of lovers' futures,
Betrayed in simple measures.
You talked, then walked, did not look back.
And I fell to knees you bastard.

I will rise up, I will declare,
My Queenhood and my power,
But for now I slump in broken parts,
A heartbreak to get over.

LULLABY

Hush little lady don't you cry,
Daddy's gone and got himself a sweeter pie.
And if that sugar's not so sweet,
Daddy's gonna get a better treat.
And hush little lady don't ask why;
This is daddy's stuff so don't you cry.

END OF MARRIAGE

A simple photo took me back,
To the place my heart had left.
The photo told a happy tale,
That leaves me now bereft.

A yearning for the better us,
With dreams of aged planning.
Where kids were young and homes were built
And we still had couple loving.

Then came the fears and cracks set firm
And alcohol brought chaos.
Where doors were smashed and ears were held
And children hid in duvets.

Where did you go and where was I?
We lost that linked connection
And here we live in homes apart
And devoid of our affection.

A life alone with kids in tow,
Is now my current walk.
My lover, friend and husband gone
And so we barely talk.

I miss the dream, the four by four,
Those golden family times,
But freedom comes at quite a price
And freedom now is mine.

Goodbye my love from yesteryear
Goodbye to half my life.
Life is tough alone for sure,
But it was so tough as your wife.

DIVORCE

Broken as one and then as two,
Witnessed the disintegration of me and you.
Tried to fix, but couldn't mix,
The ingredients of our rescue.
Mourning days of long ago,
The time ahead and the time no more.
Of present days in hell and wrath.
Crying pails, I'd cried enough.
Releasing hands, stuck with glue,
Of loyalty and kids with you.
I have to go, I know.
I have to stop. It's true.
But knowing this does not prevent,
The crushing loss of you.

CHANGES: THE BUTTERFLY AFFECT

Wings of steel, transformed to mush
In caterpillar state, I felt no rush.
The world I knew had crumpled down,
Divorce had irreparably cracked a wifey crown.

I looked to left and looked to right,
No saviour came on his steed at night.
The Surrey Hills did shield its' face,
With silent judgement, slung from grace.

I plodded, strove and quietly cracked,
Aware too well of what, or whom I lacked.
Building walls and falling down;
There goes the woman with no wifey crown.

In pupa stage I pulled tight in,
With homemade brownies and a bottle of gin.
I sobbed and broke and tore inside,
I didn't like this train wreck, rolling ride.

I stayed too long in covered state,
Aware too well of lonely fate.
The kids moved out and I stayed still,
My mindset trapped in churning mill.

From up above or somewhere else,
Came helping hands; a saving grace.
I slithered out and slowly stepped,
Though on reflection I could have leapt.

I lived, survived a terrible time.
The scars would heal; freedom was mine.
I looked behind from where I'd been,
A slow, slobbering state where I'd not been seen.

Breathing deep and praising Him,
I threw aside the empty gin (and brownie tin).
And I swore to me, as I stood there,
That these new found wings would go someplace,
somewhere.

Alone again I find myself
And the self I find is the sweetest part of
What was left behind

IT'S OK TO BE ALONE

You need a fella, you want a bloke,
Without one you say, your life is a joke.
Do not be fooled or tell yourself lies,
It's true. I know. I hear you cry.
Why?

It's ok to be alone.
With just a book and a mobile phone.

Call your friends, text some stuff;
You on your own is quite enough.
You get to choose what to do with your life.
It's fine not to be some 'one day' guy's wife.

It's ok to be alone;
In a coffee shop, with a mobile phone.

Be your own mate, go out on a date.
You get to choose, you get to say,
How to live and spend your day.

It's ok to be alone,
Just you, a book and a mobile phone.

OH DEAR

You're never too old for fear, dear.
It's never too far and it's always quite near, dear.
Stay still, stay stuck, stay on the spot,
Close all the doors and watch your life rot.

Or jump out of your way dear.
Go out and play dear.
Don't wait for another day dear.
Or life runs away dear.

LOST IN HEADSPACE

I've gone to planet cuckoo,
To the cloud above my head.
I find it helps to ground me, when
My legs they feel like lead.

I'm floating way above myself,
It's really rather cool.
Besides it stops me blabbering
And talking mummy drool.

And often when you speak to me,
I seem like I'm not here.
My eyes may glaze and head will nod,
And nothing's really clear

But I'm glad you came a'knocking;
Made up from when you call.
Just don't give up on me for I am in here,
Though it doesn't seem like it at all.

WRETCHED ANXIOUS SONG

Ripping, tearing, tugging hands that clench
Deep, inside.
Silent screams and yells and calls,
For un-sourced help.
And then I fall. Oh how I fall;
Snagging on my inner fence.

Devoid of eating, sleeping, rest.
A troubling soul failing test
after test.

Black dogs from no place, bite .
Infected poison not seen by sight.
No, I am not alright.

From whence did this feeling rise?
Not from dusty ground or clouded skies?
Not given by some other's hand,
For my disintegration into grains of sand,

But they cannot see.
For the unseen hole is deep within;
A darkened cave inside of me.

Gaping, gnawing blackness, terror,
My life feels lost whilst in this error
Of a space that has sucked me in;
A stuck place full of internal chaos and din.

I am here. Searching for the me that's gone.
Lonely; lost in this wretched anxious song.

DATING POOL

I have a list as long as my arm,
Of the guy to meet that's full of charm.
Masculine man, beardy face;
Strong, tall body and brain in place.
With money in bank and car on drive,
He's living well not on pennies to thrive.
Loving father, doting son,
Could you be my long lost one?
You'll be a lover and take me places,
Where lovers go with their desire filled faces.
Our bodies will lock and together we'll see,
Heaven on earth, yes you and me.

PANDORA'S BOX

One kiss is all it took,
To release the pain of my heart closed book.
Lips on lips in passion's embrace,
Ten years yearning betrayed on face.

Bodies lock, melt two to one;
Lips together, having fun.
Old desires flush out from deep below,
Where no other soul could go.

Just one kiss held the key,
To unlock Pandora's Box in me.
Butterflies from caverns inside
Flew out, released, no need to hide.

One kiss, there would not be more,
Butterflies come back; don't close that door.
He isn't staying he isn't steady
And I'll cry for weeks, for I wasn't ready.

I DON'T WANT YOUR MAN

Single woman don't invite!
She'll have your man for tea tonight.
Single woman leave alone,
She'll pester him with sexting phone.
Single woman, watch beware,
With her swinging hips and wavy hair.
Stay away you wanton cat.
I'll be having none of that.
You seem so sweet, but just in case,
You're not invited. You have no place.
Sorry if this seems oh so harsh,
But I'll not have my fella eye up your ass!

THE WOMAN IN OUR STREET

There's a woman in our street
That's far from meek and sweet.
She winks at all the blokes
And chortles at their jokes.

She struggles with her bins
And her lawn it needs a mow.
With willing, swinging willies,
going back and forth and fro.
(To mow her lawn, you know).

There's a woman in our street
Who doesn't have a man,
Yet Wednesday, Friday, Sunday,
Comes a fella with a van.

She has a funny job that isn't nine to five
And comes in late at night,
When I'm barely just alive.

She doesn't wear the curlers,
Or sloppy, floppy clothes.
She always has her hair done
And strikes a real, cool pose.

She tries to say hello, but I never really hear;
I'm busy with a something
And try not to get too near.

There's a woman in our street
A single mother so,
And that woman seems to cope so well,
But I really don't know how.

I do not care to know her,
For she isn't quite like me.
And besides she's rather pretty
And I'm looking fifty-three.

DIRTY FLIRTY

Hey! You said by text and word.
Such a simple, incongruous word.
Hello said I with a dot dot dot,
Thinking sweetness of which you are not.

Late at night, kids in bed,
All work was done, all words been said.
Glass in hand, my chill out time,
Then ping ping ping, my phone's alive.

Subtlety your greatest trick.
One minute hello, the next your dick.
On picture sent and I recoil.
How did I end up on sexting soil?

Perhaps I crave desire for me?
A lonely mum and a bed roomy.
Subconscious wants for bodily needs,
Led to others wanton greed.

My instincts scream, 'Stop this stuff!'
Can't you see, you've seen enough?
It's just a game and you'll not win,
Pretending sex is just a whim.

And when all is said and all is done
And the two have satiated meaningless fun,
Regret and shame a stain will stay
And tomorrow you're single another day.

BLOW OUT

Sitter booked, broke a nail,
My hair a mess, my temper flails.
I'm rushing out and kids want kisses,
But I'm tight on time and don't want to miss this.
First date is on and I've dressed up,
Did my hair, nails, waxed and all that stuff.
What shall I wear, I cry aloud,
To a confused under ten watching crowd.

'You look pretty in pink' says girl 2,
'No you don't, wear some blue'.
Says boy who's four and covered in glue.
'Oh no you don't!' I grab his mess.
I wash him down, try not to stress.

Sitter here and I relax,
Grab a wine, pour at least one glass.
And so I breathe and finally smile,
For this first date, I've run a mile.
But he's cute and beardy; just my type.
I'll soon be sitting with a guy called Mike.

Taxi comes and off I go,
Leaving chaos at the door.
I arrive in time with minutes to spare.
I slide on in and find a chair.
Beside the bar and choose to wait.
It's usually me who's running late.

A drink I buy and play with phone,
Not thinking of the kids at home.
A text I sent, then three or four,
As I keep on glancing at the door.

Ten minutes gone and then it's thirty.
My thoughts are sadness instead of dirty.
Forty minutes come and go,
I sigh, get up and head for the door.

A man walks in as I walk out.
He smiles at me but I just pout.
I don't care if Brad Pitt walked in,
I'm going home to drink some gin.

My eyes are older, my head more wise
These are sunset not sunrise days.
Your smile, your warmth, it fills my heart
That came back after it's sad depart.

SECOND CHANCES

When I wasn't looking,
When sites were off, not seen,
When I resigned to oneness,
You came and you found me.

You sidled up beside me
And oh it felt so right,
To meet you at the counter
With my teabags, ham and tights.

'Hello' you said and smiled
And your mouth split ear from ear.
I didn't want to hide,
So instead I drew quite near.

'I saw you in the café
But I don't think you saw me?
I like their cakes and homemade scones
And they make good, strong coffee.'

'Yes!' I think I muttered
And my heart it beat a drum,
And my hands they got all sweaty ,
As I tried to suck in my tum.

'I've seen you round I offered'
And my eyes they locked on his,
But then I looked into his basket
Ten pound meal for two, plus fizz.

Oh! I sighed and wilted;
This guy is not for me.
I like him, Oh I do,
But that's not dinner set for three.

He saw my eyes a linger, on
His salmon en-croute and beans.
And then he looked into my own;
Lonely meal for one it seemed.

'No plans tonight?' He offered
And I saddened at the mock.
How I wished that opportunity
Would stop at just the knock.

'A quiet night in tonight' I said,
My face in flush I knew,
And he placed his lips beside my ear
And whispered ,'Yes me too!'

'This is for my neighbours;
They're elderly you see.
She is 82 and he is 83.
They celebrate their love, of over 60 years
And when I said I'd treat them this,
They both let out some tears.

She has got the cancer
And his legs don't work no more.
It's the least that I could do for them,
As I only live next door.

'Oh!' I said 'How lovely!'
And I meant it with delight,
Suddenly his latter words
Made my beating heart alight.

'I know this is so forward
And I know it's quite a cheek,
But I wonder if you'll share with me,
A supper one day next week?'

He said this with a charming grin
And I found I did declare,
'I'm free tonight, if you like?'
And that was yesteryear.

And our years have grown so fast
And our hearts together fond.
To think we met in aisle no 3,
Instead of the fishy dating pond.

TWO MANY WOMEN

A gaggle of geese,
A waddle of chicks,
All bits are tucked in,
No wobbling dicks.
Loud, non-stop talking,
Over wine or some tea;
Champagne is worse,
Especially with three.
Everything covered,
From you, me and them;
Politics, weight and the sulphites in ham.
Loving your dress,
Coveting your shoes,
Gossiping and gaggling
Over yesterday's news.
Measuring, judging, comparing and all,
We're not competing, just saying, that's all.
I love all my friends,
I love all their stuff,
But sometimes
Alone time,
By myself, is enough.

THE BIG 5-OH

I've gone and hit the big 5 Oh!
Oh crap, I'm not so young no more.
Kids are growing and need me less;
My life devoid of childhood mess.
It's samey same with my balding spouse,
Who goes to work and returns a mouse.
His middle life feels so dim
I know I could be losing him.
So I've started yoga and joined a gym
Anything to get me trim.

Sex is stale and nothing new,
But I want to spend my life with you.
So what please tell me, should I do?

My bottom drawer has a buzzy thing
And I've dress up clothes just for him,
But my breasts they sag and my tummy too
And my boring clothes make me blue.
But yet I want to spend my life with you.

And then you say some rainy day,
'I'm tired of this, I want more play.'
Quietly I shiver and await the words,
'I'm off to find some younger birds.'
But no, instead you pull me tight,
Kiss me firm and inside I light.

'I love you girl, let's go upstairs,
I don't want to leave or have sex in pairs.
I don't need toys or things to watch,
With moans and groans and a shaven crotch.
To run away to another's arms,
To be seduced by wicked charms.
It's you I want and all of you.
Not something fresh, or someone new.
Let's go upstairs and play our tricks.
Then we'll make some lunch and watch Netflix.'

SHE'S A TENOR LADY

Don't make me laugh, or cough or run.
Sudden movement is no longer fun.
Doing a jig, or a jog or a jive,
Used to make me feel alive.
Trampolining is a scary task,
I'll politely decline if you so much as ask.

Where once I sang in soprano voice,
My loss of functions, leaves little choice.
No I'm afraid those days are gone,
And now I'm singing the Tenor lady song.

MENOPAUSAL ME

I've gone a little crazy, I cannot tell you why.
I'm up at night all sweaty and periods all went 'bye.'

I've feeling rather moody, as if you couldn't tell,
Moody is such a soft sweet word, for emotions that
came from hell.

I'm feeling hot and flushy, my face tomato red
And if you pause to mention it, I'll hit you round the
head.

I'm feeling rather dry, in places down below,
But I'm still up for relations, in case you have to know.

I'm feeling kinda sad, for the womb that has now gone;
Embracing new beginnings and accepting this new song.

I'm learning to adapt and welcome in this tide,
Of brand new crazy me, but yet I want to hide.

To go back to being young, when my body was so fresh.
Not this aching, sweaty, flushy me; a madly menopausal
mess.

I'M FINE REALLY. MARK 3

Sixty-eight and just me and him.
Grandkids around me keeping me trim.
Friends that I see for tea and a chat,
Sometimes we get merry and do things like that.
It's fine; all's fine.

Then one day I awake with a feeling inside,
My left breast is bumpy and we go for a ride
To the doctor whose face wears a look of concern,
And a mammogram's booked. I've so much to learn.
Hospitals, corridors, hard, cold machines,
That squash up your breasts and leave you in tears.
I'm fine really. Just fine.

Scans and biopsies, appointments galore,
Waiting for doctor to walk through that door.
Look at his features for clues on my fate,
Scared of the words, yet still cannot wait.
You're fine. Just fine. The lump is benign.

I don't feel elated, don't feel so brave,
Knowing one foot was left in the grave.

MY PHONE CALL QUEEN

When low or high, or lost between,
You are my go to phone call queen.
When all alone or somewhat stressed,
It's you I call, when I'm a mess.
Your voice or text or emoji grin,
Calms my soul and quietens the din.
I know that I am free to be all of me,
When I call can call my phone call queen.

FUNNY LITTLE BESTIE

My funny little bestie,
With flat boobs and big round bum.
With eyes to fill a goldfish bowl
And the cutest tiny tum.

My funny little bestie,
Who calls a spade a brush,
And doesn't care for speaking loud,
Prefers a gossipy hush.

Oh funny little bestie,
Who never leaves my side.
Who made me be her bridesmaid
When she was shotgun bride.

Sweet funny little bestie,
Of two she is a mum,
But she'll always be the girl who peed herself,
When we had too much fun!

WOMEN IN ARMS

Nothing like another lass to link your arms up to,
To form a woman chain of friends when
You're sad, in need or blue.
Women friends are awesome.
They cackle, cheer, uphold
And tell you if your bum's too big,
Or your tum needs extra hold.
They are great to have a tea with,
Or a glass of wine or two,
And when you're at a loose end,
They'll come and shop with you.
But beware when full moon rises,
And if your friends are near;
It's bloated bellies and tampon time
And 'woman time' my dear.

LADIES WHO LUNCH

We talk of china cups and pots; of Doris' new 'do.
You said you liked it better grey than that wicked
purple hue.
We speak aloud to hear ourselves, above the teashop
din.
I remembered my false teeth today, but the hearing
aid isn't in.
You compliment my flowery dress and I welcome in your
shoes.
Then we gossip about all the topics that are making
daily news.
Oooh you say and Ahh I go and this goes on a while.
Till the young man asks us what we want and we give him
such a smile.

You choose the soup, with doorstep bread and I choose
cheese and ham
And we chortle laugh together as we recall those tins
of spam.
Friends and husbands, here and gone are all within our
chat
And when we're spent on those, we're discussing your
black cat.

The man returns with lunch and we ooh and ahh again.
I ask for a spot of mustard, as soup drops on your chin.
A tattooed girl walks in with a top that's barely there
And I find that we've gone quiet as we're trying not to
stare.

For thirty years we've been doing this;
Meeting to share some tea.
We know our quirks and movements;
It makes us feel quite free.

Most of our life is over, but there's more left in the
bag.
Our hearing's going, our teeth are false and yes, we
often nag.
But these are blissful moments, ones we love and
treasure.
With our granny shoes, flowery prints and perms,
We're doing this life together.

MUMMY ROLLS AND FLABBY STUFF

Muffin tops and doughy thighs,
Saggy breasts and nothing high.
South they went and didn't look back
And I am not okay with that.

Greying hair and wrinkly lines,
Ageing spots are just not fine.
Chicken neck and thinning lips,
Widening girth along with hips.

Flopping ears and lengthening nose
And funny hairs, what's with all those,
Hairs on chin and some in ears?
Frankly they have to go my dear.

Chunky knees with wrinkles smiling,
Cracks on face, that require tiling.
Aching back and corn hard toes,
Not looking right in most my clothes.

But heck I've lived and had a ball.
Stuff the yellowing teeth and all.
The wine I drank and those wild girl times,
The G&T, champagne and wine.

Days at Ascot, Henley too,
And I did them all with them or you.
Trips abroad in ageing sun,
Oh but wasn't it all so much fun?

No longer young I'll give you that.
No longer kitten, more like fat cat.
But I lived a life and lived it well
And I wear the marks, can't you tell?

Looking into the pond I see me
Not the one in my head
But the one in the water.
Who is this wrinkled prune looking
back at me?
That's not the me I see.

SAYING GOODBYE

Dear Mum, you broke my heart.
I wasn't ready for your depart.
One day alive, the next no more,
No time to walk you to the door.

Goodbye sweet mother, bestest friend.
Will this crushing sorrow ever end?
No more calls or trips to shops.
All that joy with you has stopped.

Farewell to the deepest part of me.
Your heart was weak and we could not see.
And now mine aches and is torn apart,
Awaiting healing that may never start.

I SEE YOU

In he walks and I scan the room.
Did anyone hear my heart go boom?
Soft, flicky hair, teeth so white;
Oh to take him home tonight.
Bright blue eyes of crystal, gaze
Upon the rainbow cakes on trays.
Victoria Sponge, Lemon Drizzle,
He licks his lips and my insides fizzle.
Tee shirt white and off it would come,
With my weathered hands on his pert little bum.
He's in his thirties I reckon so,
I've walked the boards enough to know.
He smiles at me this handsome chap,
With him around, I'd never nap.
I offer back a toothy grin,
So pleased my teeth are all back in.

I'm shrunken now, my legs are old.
My chest it suffers from the cold.
My hair is white, the wrinkles firm
And my pelvic floor is now infirm.
He smiles because he sees a gran
And I grin back at this young man.

This old girl of eighty-three,
Isn't whom I really see.
Inside my head I'm twenty-two
And I would take a walk with you.
Beside a lake, in woods or beach,
So much to learn, so much to teach.
Together you and I would laugh, have liaisons,
Argue, cry.
The thought of it makes me sigh.

But then a crumb gets stuck in my throat;
I drop my fork and then my coat.
I cough, I wee but I've got a pad.
Then you look away and I am sad.

WHERE HAVE ALL MY TEA FRIENDS GONE?

Betty went, her legs were bad,
Though she swore a lot so I weren't too sad.
Jim he smoked, thirty a day;
Couldn't keep the reaper at bay.
He coughed and then he coughed no more.
Doris too went out that door.
Elsie made me laugh with glee,
The jokes she told that made me pee!
Two years ago she left this earth;
I'll miss those tears that came with mirth.
Anne was sweet, just like a mouse.
Sad when her coffin left her house.
Tony, John and Dai the Beer.
Let's not mention him my dear!
Frankie, Ed and Millie too;
How I wish to tea with you.
But now I sit and all alone,
No one to meet, no one to phone.
I've kept so fit in all these years,
Not smoked, nor drank or drown in tears.
A happy soul, my heart was light.
A lived a life and I lived it right.
But husband died a while ago
And kids they rarely come and go.
And friends they lie in pastures new,
So it's tea for one, not tea for two.

I HAD A BLAST

I've seen a lot and kept some safe,
In a little inside me, hidey place.
Looking demure, with highway'd skin;
I've secrets hidden like my rhubarb gin.

You'll not get me to talk.
Tight lipped and memory as crumbling chalk.
But there was a guy some moons ago,
I kissed whilst standing in the snow.
Alf was away on business trip
And the naughty part of me let rip.

Ah those days of long ago,
The secrets I take with me right now.
As I lay on my gurney bed,
With sheets of white, just like my head.
Alf has gone so long ago
And that fella from the kiss in snow.

I'm ready though, so don't be sad.
My life has not been oh so bad.
I've seen a lot and kept some safe,
Inside my little hidey place.
And that place will stay with me for now,
As I say goodbye and take a bow.

I'M FINE REALLY. MARK 4

Words of wisdom I will bestow
On all who want to hear.
Come hither young and old alike,
Come closer and come near.

Life is long and then it's short;
It's just the way it goes.
So take these words into your heart
And right down to your toes.

Beware regret and anger too,
Unforgiveness is like dry rot.
Let go of pain and all that's blue,
Live life with all you've got.

Laugh loud and hard until you wee
And your tummy hurts like hell.
Laughter lines are beautiful child,
So wear them proud as well.

Smile with eyes as well as mouth
And let the joy outshine;
Any sadness in your heart,
That hasn't healed with time.

Take a lover or take two,
When marriages come and go
And do not be afraid to love,
Until the right one has found you.

Give and give and give some more,
For it will all come back.
Life is really wasted,
On focusing on lack.

And finally I say to you,
And all who want to know,
Go out, live, laugh, achieve your dreams,
Enjoy life's rock and roll.

Paula Love Clark

Printed in Poland
by Amazon Fulfillment
Poland Sp. z o.o., Wrocław